ollins Revised

Engaging English 4

Workbook

Ruby Bose

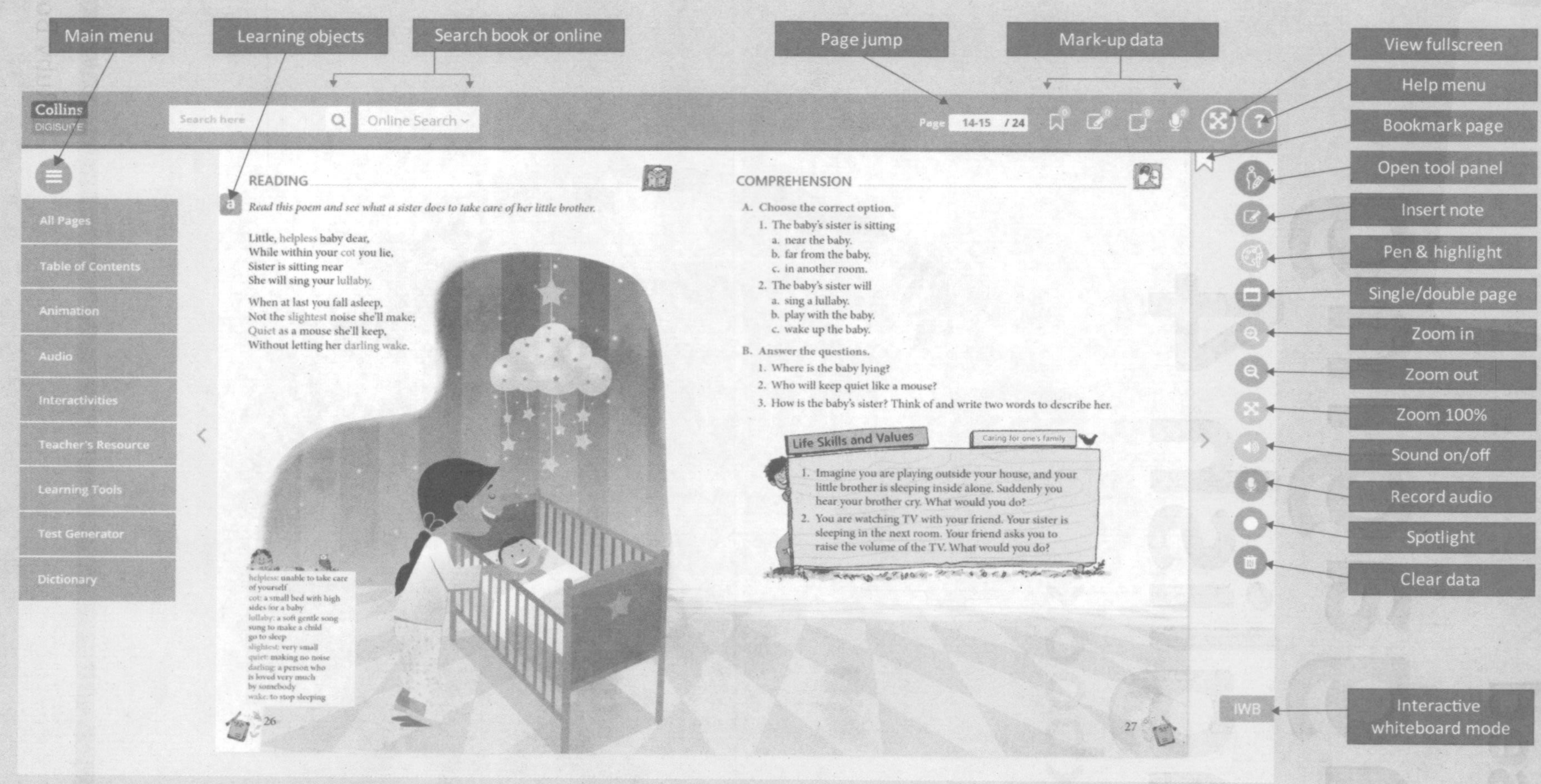

Student + Teacher

a animations

ilt instructor-led tutorials

ia activities

w worksheets

audio

g games

v videos

Teacher-only

lp lesson plans

w worksheets

tn teacher's notes

ak answer keys

Preface

Revised Engaging English aims to instill an appreciation for literature in today's learners, while equipping them with the tools to develop native fluency and communicative competence in using the English language. The eight-level series comprises Coursebooks, Workbooks, and digital resources for teachers for all levels.

The revised edition has been aligned closely with the guidelines of the National Education Policy, 2020 through its focus on twenty-first century skills, Sustainable Development Goals (SDGs), cross-curricular learning, 'Happiness' content and art-integrated learning. Coursebooks and Workbooks 1 and 2 integrate the essence of NIPUN (National Initiative for Proficiency in Reading with Understanding and Numeracy). They aim to motivate students to read independently, improve their vocabulary, develop their critical thinking and creative skills and enhance their ability to express themselves verbally and in writing.

The lessons are built around carefully selected literary pieces with distinct cross-curricular themes, and presented with glossary, explanation of literary terms and interesting trivia. The end-of-chapter exercises address the needs of formal language learning.

The **Workbooks** are designed to complement the Coursebooks, by providing additional skills practice, review and assessments. They comprise the following sections:

Comprehension includes factual, inferential and evaluative questions based on short reading passages.

Way with Words includes exercises on the vocabulary topics encountered in the Coursebook as well as extension activities derived from it. It also incorporates activities on literary devices and figures of speech, spelling drills and exercises on dictionary usage.

Grammar in Use starts with a short explanation of important grammar concepts covered in the Coursebook, followed by plenty of practice for reinforcement.

Listening and Speaking builds students' oral and aural communication skills. It includes tasks such as phonics drills, conversation practice, role plays and debates to develop spoken English skills. Listening comprehension exercises teach students to listen for both general and specific details. In poetry chapters, there are activities on stress, rhyme and metre.

Pen it Down: The activities in this section include guided and free writing tasks derived from the reading text, which build on the functional and creative writing skills of the learner.

Each Workbook also contains two **Tests**. One of these is based on the principle of SAFAL (Structured Assessment For Analyzing Learning), a competency-based assessment introduced by CBSE. They assess the competencies of critical thinking as well as inquiry-based and analysis-based learning. The other test is modelled on class assessments.

The series encourages competency-based education which allows concept acquisition at the learner's own pace, based on individual ability. We hope that it will foster a love for literature and reading in young learners.

Detailed Contents

Unit	Theme	Way with Words	Grammar in Use	Listening and Speaking	Pen it Down
10. Oliver Goes to London	The City	• Synonyms • Suffixes: *-ind* and *-ild*	• Prepositions • Transitive and intransitive verbs	• Listening comprehension: retelling a story	• Character sketch • Writing a short composition: predicting the ending of a story
11. The Naga Dragon's Lair	Southeast Asia	• Similes • Matching objects with their colours	• Types of adjectives • Types of adverbs	• Listening comprehension: fill in the blanks	• Writing a personal account
12. The Sound Collector	Daily Activities	• Onomatopoeic words • Imagery	• Tenses	• Listening comprehension: identifying sounds	• Paragraph writing
13. The Wizard of Oz	Long Journeys	• Anagrams	• Phrases • Apostrophe to show possession	• Listening comprehension: rhyming words	• Poster making
14. The Lighthouse	By the Sea	• Forming new words by adding a letter	• Present and past participles	• Words with silent letters	• Making an invitation card
15. How the Leopard Got His Spots	Animal Stories	• Word grid: animal names • Suffix • Abbreviations	• Adjective phrases	• Listening comprehension: sequencing	• Researching and writing a short paragraph
16. The Girl Who Stepped on the Loaf	Christmas Stories	• Matching pictures with names • Word grid : antonyms • Crossword: plural forms of nouns	• Direct and indirect speech • Error correction	• Conversation: speaking on a given topic	• Story writing
17. My Elephant is Missing	Humour	• Matching objects with the places they are kept in • Homonyms	• Apostrophe for contractions	• Soft and hard *th*	• Notice writing
18. Harriet and the Underground Railroad	Freedom and Slavery	• Idioms • Collocations • Matching nouns and verbs	• Subject-verb agreement • Conjunctions	• Giving a speech	• E-mail writing
Assessment (SAFAL)					

Contents

1

Heidi

Way with Words

Collective Nouns

A **collective noun** is used to talk about a group of persons, animals or things taken as a whole.

Examples: A **crew** of sailors
A **pile** of books

A. Complete these collective nouns by choosing the correct words from the box.

soldiers	lions	monkeys	wolves	bees
birds	sheep	ships	elephants	whales

1. a pack of ____________
2. a fleet of ____________
3. a herd of ____________
4. an army of ____________
5. a pride of ____________
6. a flock of ____________
7. a troop of ____________
8. a flight of ____________
9. a school of ____________
10. a swarm of ____________

B. Make sentences with the collective nouns from the above exercise.

1. ____________
2. ____________
3. ____________

4. ____

5. ____

6. ____

7. ____

8. ____

9. ____

10. ____

Grammar in Use

Types of Sentences

You have learnt that there are four types of sentences.

An **assertive sentence** says or states something.

Example: I am eating an apple.

An **interrogative sentence** asks a question.

Example: Do you stay in this house?

An **exclamatory sentence** expresses a strong emotion.

Example: Oh, what a beautiful dress she is wearing!

An **imperative sentence** gives an order or makes a request.

Example: Please close the door.

A. Identify whether the following sentences are assertive (A), imperative (I), interrogative (In) or exclamatory (E). One is done for you.

1. *I have ten rupees.* A
2. Where shall we go for a picnic? ________
3. Hurray, we won the race! ________
4. Tie your shoelaces. ________
5. The sky is blue. ________
6. Come here. ________
7. When do we leave? ________
8. Ouch, I cut my finger! ________

B. Complete these sentences.

1. I have ____.
2. What ____?
3. Wow, ____!
4. Today we will ____.
5. Please, ____.
6. How ____?
7. Alas, ____!
8. Are we ____?
9. It is ____.
10. Go ____.

Adjectives

You know that adjectives are describing words.
Example: Heidi awoke the next morning to a **shrill** whistle.

C. Match the adjectives in Column A with the nouns in Column B.

Adjectives	Nouns
1. careless	a. chair
2. famous	b. sky
3. hardworking	c. child
4. cloudy	d. mistake
5. ancient	e. student
6. adorable	f. actor
7. kind	g. monument
8. comfortable	h. morning
9. dull	i. teacher

D. Form adjectives from these nouns by adding suitable endings. One is done for you.

1. *sun* *sunny*
2. wool ____________
3. rain ____________
4. luck ____________
5. brown ____________
6. danger ____________
7. value ____________
8. history ____________

Listening and Speaking

A. These words in each pair sound the same but have different meanings. Now, listen to some sentences being read aloud and from each set, underline the word that has been used in the sentence.

1. ate	eight
2. sale	sail
3. wait	weight
4. hole	whole
5. flour	flower
6. rows	rose
7. be	bee
8. waist	waste

B. Work in pairs. Take turns to tell your partner about what you like. Give reasons for your choices. You may use the following points to help you speak:

- What do you like to do in your free time?
- Why do you like it?
- What are its advantages and disadvantages?
- Have you faced any problems because of it?
- Are you happy about your choice?

Pen it Down

Imagine yourself to be Heidi and write a diary entry about the first day you spent in the mountains.

You can include points like:

- what you had expected
- what all you saw
- your feelings

2

A Noble Dog

Way with Words

Antonyms and Synonyms

Synonyms are words that have the same meaning.

Example: sad–unhappy

Antonyms are words that have opposite meanings.

Example: absent–present

A. Look at the word pairs. Write S for synonyms and A for antonyms.

1. wet–dry: ☐
2. appear–disappear: ☐
3. before–after: ☐
4. scared–afraid: ☐
5. awake–asleep: ☐

B. Read the words given in the two boxes. Choose the correct synonyms and antonyms for the words in the table. One is done for you.

synonyms

huge strong useful
pretty quick joyful

antonyms

unhappy unhelpful soft
ugly small slow

Words	Synonyms	Antonyms
1. beautiful	*pretty*	*ugly*
2. big		
3. fast		
4. happy		
5. hard		
6. helpful		

Grammar in Use

Simple Past Tense

Read these sentences.

I **play** with my friends everyday.
I **played** football with my cousins yesterday.

The first sentence describes an action that happens daily. The second sentence talks about something that has already happened. Therefore, the verb **played** is in the simple past tense.

The **simple past tense** is used to describe an event that has already taken place.

We usually form this tense by adding *-d* or *-ed* to the base verb.

A. Make sentences in the simple past tense to describe these pictures. One is done for you.

1.

2.

3.

4.

5.

6.
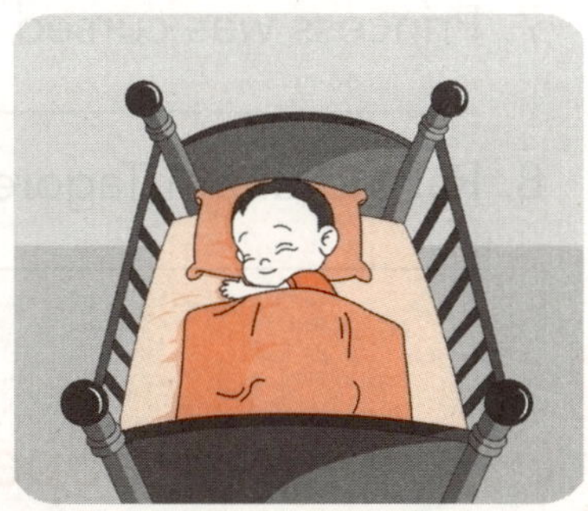

1. *My father cooked dinner last night.*
2. Rajan ____________________.
3. The children ____________________.
4. Sonia ____________________.
5. Grandma ____________________.
6. The baby ____________________.

ARTICLES

You know that **a, an** and **the** are called **articles.**

A and **an** are **indefinite articles** as they do not point or refer to any specific person or thing.

Example: We saw **a** butterfly in the garden. (any butterfly)
He had **an** orange for breakfast. (no specific orange)

A is used before words that begin with a consonant or a consonant sound.

Examples: **a** table, **a** cup, **a** university

An is used before words that begin with a vowel or a vowel sound.

Examples: **an** umbrella, **an** ink pot, **an** hour

The is the **definite article** as it points or refers to a specific person or thing.

Example: My uncle met **the** director of the company. (a specific person)

B. Rewrite the sentences inserting articles wherever necessary.

1. I dropped vase when I heard noise.

   ____

2. We went for walk along bank of river.

   ____

3. Rhea is good artist.

   ____

4. Raman took cloth and wiped wet plates.

   ____

5. There is banyan tree behind my house.

   ____

6. Joy saw bag lying on pavement.

   ____

7. Princess was cursed by wicked magician.

   ____

8. Rabindranath Tagore wrote national anthem of India.

   ____

Listening and Speaking

Work in pairs. Take turns with your partner to read out these words. Say the letters in bold with more stress.

water	**car**toon	**may**be
better	**car**ton	**peo**ple
parent	**stu**dent	**sam**ple
table	**num**ber	**rai**ny

Pen it Down

A. If you had a puppy, what would you do to take good care of it? Write all the things you would do in the boxes. One is done for you.

I would keep it clean.

I have a puppy. Its name is ____________ .

B. Now, write a paragraph describing your puppy and its features and habits. Mention what you love about it the most.

3

Grandad's Gadget

Way with Words

Compound Words

You have learnt that when two separate words are joined to make a new word, they form a **compound word**.

A. Match the words in columns A and B to form new words. One is done for you.

A	B	
1. foot	a. fire	1. *footprint*
2. camp	b. cake	2. ______
3. pan	c. port	3. ______
4. birth	d. word	4. ______
5. rain	e. print	5. ______
6. air	f. wash	6. ______
7. white	g. day	7. ______
8. pass	h. coat	8. ______

Professions

B. People from different professions have often invented things that changed the world. Match these famous inventors named in Column A with their inventions listed in Column B.

Column A	Column B
1. Thomas Edison	a. printing press
2. Johannes Gutenberg	b. World Wide Web
3. James Naismith	c. telephone
4. Tim Berners-Lee	d. light bulb
5. Alexander Graham Bell	e. basketball

Grammar in Use

Pronouns

You have learnt that a **pronoun** is a word that is used in place of a noun.

A **personal pronoun** is used to indicate people or things.

Examples: **I** wake up early everyday.
He goes to school on time.
She tells me a story at night.

A pronoun used as the subject of a verb is called a **subject pronoun**. These are *I*, *you* (singular and plural), *he*, *she*, *it*, *they*, and *we*.

A pronoun used as the object of a verb is called an **object pronoun**. These are *me*, *you*, *him*, *her*, *it*, *them*, and *us*.

A. Choose the correct pronouns to complete the sentences.

1. ____________ am eating an apple. (You/I)
2. Are ____________ crying? (he/you)
3. ____________ are watching a play. (We/She)
4. ____________ is raining very heavily today. (You/It)
5. ____________ is helping his father in the kitchen. (It/He)
6. ____________ are planting trees in the garden. (They/I)

B. Complete the sentences with suitable pronouns.

1. My sister and I have a cupboard. ____________ is a big cupboard.
2. Is German a difficult language? Yes, ____________ is.
3. The children on the bus are waving at us. ____________ know them.
4. My uncle and aunt live in China. ____________ often visit us.
5. I have a pet dog. ____________ is two years old.
6. Ali is watching television. ____________ is watching a cricket match.
7. My cousins do not live in India. ____________ are studying abroad.
8. The soldier fled from the battlefield. ____________ was punished.

Punctuation

Read these sentences.

piya are you going to the library on saturday

Piya, are you going to the library on Saturday?

The second sentence makes complete sense because the punctuation marks are used correctly.

Punctuation marks are used to help make the meaning of a sentence clear to the reader. They include the comma, full stop, question mark, exclamation mark and capital letters.

C. Rewrite the sentences using proper punctuation.

1. i have a pet dog

____

2. stop the thief

____

3. how are you mohan

____

4. what a beautiful kite

____

5. farah is the class monitor

____

6. ritika, my friend, is a painter

____

7. do you know that girl playing in the field

____

8. hurrah we have come first in the competition

____

9. my brother loves to eat chocolate

____

10. the cat with the bushy tail belongs to my aunt

____

Listening and Speaking

Do these words have a soft 'c' sound as in 'ice' or a hard 'c' sound as in 'cat'? Say them aloud and write them in the correct columns.

pencil   fence   carrot   corn   face   cart   scissors   canoe   dice   cookie

Soft *c* as in *ice*	Hard *c* as in *cat*

Pen it Down

Imagine that your friend has helped you repair an expensive toy that you accidentally broke. Write a 'thank you' note to your friend for his/her help. You may use the following phrases in your note:

- Thank you for...
- If it weren't for you...
- This toy is very special...
- I will always remember...
- Now we can play...

A BIG thank you!

Dear ______________, (write your friend's name here)

Thank you so much for ______________________________

Lots of love,

______________ (write your name here)

4

Guno and Koyo

Comprehension

Read the passage and answer the questions.

A rumour was doing the rounds in the ancient kingdom of Vijayanagara. It was believed that the old man Ramayya, who lived with his wife in a hut just outside the walls of the city, was cursed. Anyone who looked at the man's face would immediately lose their appetite and would go hungry. People were terrified of Ramayya and avoided him like the plague.

King Sri Krishnadevaraya learnt about this and decided to find out the truth. The next day, he called his guards and asked them to make Ramayya spend the night in the room located to the right of his royal bedchamber. Then he could see Ramayya's face as soon as he woke up in the morning.

The soldiers followed Krishnadevaraya's orders. The king saw Ramayya's face as soon as he woke up and looked into the room next to his bedchamber.

Soon the king sat down to have his breakfast. Suddenly, he noticed an insect in one of the dishes. He told the cooks to prepare him a fresh breakfast spread. By the time they brought in the rich feast, the king had lost his appetite.

This made Krishnadevaraya believe that Ramayya was responsible for the loss of his appetite. He became extremely angry and ordered the guards to hang the old man.

Ramayya's wife heard this news and begged the courtier Tenali Raman to help her husband. Raman patiently heard her story and decided to help her.

The following morning, Tenali Raman went to Ramayya and said something in his ear that no one else could hear. The old man was being taken to be hanged, but before they could go any further, he exclaimed, 'Stop! I have a final wish before I die. Surely the just king will grant a dying man's last wish.' On being asked what it was, Ramayya replied, 'My wish is that this note be given to our king before I am put to death.'

The guards gave the note to the king. On the note were the words that were whispered by Tenali Raman. It said, 'If a person loses his appetite after looking at Ramayya's face, then after looking at the king's face, one will lose his life. Therefore, which man is more cursed, Ramayya or the king?'

When the king read the note, he was ashamed and sorry for his foolishness. He ordered the guards to set Ramayya free at once.

A. Complete the sentences with suitable words from the passage.

1. The name of the king was ________________.
2. At breakfast, the king spotted an ____________ in one of the dishes.
3. The king had looked at ________________ face in the morning.
4. The old man's wife asked ______________ to help her.
5. The king realised his ____________ after reading the note.

B. Tick the correct answer.

1. Ramayya lived

a. outside the forest   b. outside the walls of the city   c. in a village

2. If people looked at Ramayya's face, they would lose

a. their eyesight   b. their life   c. their appetite

3. The king sat at the table to eat

a. breakfast   b. dinner   c. lunch

4. The note was given to the king before Ramayya was to be

a. hanged   b. put in the prison   c. released

C. Read the line from the passage and answer the questions.

'Stop! I have a final wish...'

1. Who said these words?

____

2. What was the speaker's last wish?

____

3. What was written in the note?

____

4. What happened when the king read the note?

____

5. What lesson did you learn from the story?

____

E S J G

Way with Words

PROVERBS

A **proverb** is a short, popular saying that generally expresses a truth or gives advice.

Example: A friend in need is a friend indeed.

A. Match the groups of words in Columns A and B to complete the proverbs.

Column A	Column B
1. A bird in hand	a. change its spots
2. A journey of a thousand miles	b. is the devil's workshop
3. A leopard cannot	c. gathers no moss
4. Always put your	d. is worth two in a bush
5. An idle brain	e. best foot forward
6. A picture is worth	f. begins with a single step
7. A rolling stone	g. so you shall reap
8. As you sow,	h. a thousand words

Phrasal Verbs

When a verb is used with a preposition or an adverb to mean something different from their separate meanings, it is called a **phrasal verb**.

Example: **Turn down** the music. It is too loud.

B. Complete the sentences with the correct form of the phrasal verbs given in the box.

bring out	break down	carry on
call off	look after	turn up

1. The car __________ on its way to the airport.
2. We shall soon __________ the school newsletter.
3. The workers __________ their strike when their demands were met.
4. Ravi __________ reading his book even after the lights were switched off.
5. Our uncle __________ us when our parents were away.
6. More than fifty people __________ for the party.

Grammar in Use

Subject and Predicate

The **subject** of a sentence names the person or thing that we speak about.

The **predicate** tells us something about the subject.

Example: *Carla* (subject) kicked the football with all her might. (predicate).

A. Underline the subjects and circle the predicates in the sentences. One is done for you.

1. Robin and Reema (played football in the rain.)
2. The naughty children ran about in the corridor.
3. Mummy threw the rotten apples into the dustbin.
4. The hungry tiger chased the rabbit.
5. The mango was very sweet.
6. The big brown bear growled at the fox.
7. We will play in the park today.
8. The car raced past us at great speed.
9. Batman is my favourite superhero.

WORD FORMS: ADJECTIVES TO NOUNS

B. Complete the sentences with the noun form of the adjectives in brackets.

1. Ravi got a reward from his teacher because of his ____________. (honest)
2. I don't want to face my science teacher's ____________, so I will submit the project on time. (angry)
3. The ____________ drive started by our school was successful. (clean)
4. Rina can't sleep alone at night because of her fear of ____________. (dark)
5. We must always maintain ____________ in the library. (silent)
6. The doctor informed us that the patient was out of ____________. (dangerous)
7. The king ruled well and was loved by all because of his ____________. (wise)

INVERTED COMMA

Inverted commas are used to mark the beginning and end of the words of a speaker. In such sentences, the inverted commas are placed after punctuation marks like full stop, question marks and exclamation marks.

Example: The plumber said, 'I can repair the tap in no time!'

C. Rewrite the sentences after putting the inverted commas in the right places. Remember to punctuate the sentences correctly.

1. Grandma said Maya, why are you so sad.

   ____

2. Rohan asked Ma'am can you please explain the question again.

   ____

3. Tina said Mum, I am going out to play.

   ____

4. Varun said do you like chocolate.

   ____

5. Hurray we won the children exclaimed.

   ____

6. Subna said let us go and watch a film at the theatre.

____

7. Do you know where Sana is? Neha asked.

____

Listening and Speaking

A. Practise these dialogues with your partner. Notice the highlighted words in the conversation.

Situation 1

Person 1: **Would you like to** join us for dinner tonight?

Person 2: Thank you. **That would be nice**.

Situation 2

Person 1: **Are you joining us** for the picnic?

Person 2: Sorry, **I am busy**.

Situation 3

Person 1: **Shall we** go for a holiday together?

Person 2: Yes, **that would be lovely**.

B. Now, enact a situation in which you invite your friend for lunch. Your friend may either decide to come for lunch, or refuse, and explain the reason for the decision.

Pen it Down

Imagine that you are the Hadji. Write a diary entry, narrating your experience on the night Guno and Koyo came to rob your house. You may use the following phrases in your note:

- woken from sleep by a noise
- discovering the hole in the wall
- relieved to find all valuables safe
- joining the chase to catch the robbers

____

____

____

____

5 Bread Making

Comprehension

Read the passage and answer the questions.

It is very difficult to say which is the best cuisine in the world. Each cuisine has its own flavours and methods of preparing a dish. However, we can certainly talk about the most popular foods in the world. It is possible to discuss about national dishes, cultural food, and the most desired and famous foods in the world.

As a matter of fact, each country has some unique foods which may have come from another country located far away. For example, the Bahn Mi sandwich, a very popular street food in Vietnam, was brought to the country by the country's French rulers in the past.

Pizza is the most popular food in the whole world, especially in the USA. It was brought to the country by Italians who arrived between 1880 and 1920. Today, we can buy a pizza in almost every city in the world, and it is believed that almost 350 slices of pizza are eaten every second. A pizza is made of a flattened round dough topped with cheese, fresh tomato sauce and canned meat, fish, or vegetables. It may be garnished with basil, olives, and oregano. Sometimes a dash of olive oil is also added. Based on the toppings, among the most famous types of Italian pizza are Margherita and Napolitana.

The Italian pizza might be considered the most-loved food in the world, but a close second is the Turkish doner kebab. This popular street food can be found almost everywhere in the world. Traditionally, doner kebab is made of Turkish *pide* bread filled with marinated and grilled mutton, lamb or chicken, lettuce, tomatoes and onions.

These days, a lot of people also enjoy sushi, which originated in Japan. Bite-sized pieces of fish or other seafood, often raw, are served over a bed of flavoured rice and are topped with the paste of a spicy root vegetable called wasabi. People started eating the modern version of sushi in Japan in the 1820s. Japan is made up of islands, and so a wide selection of seafood is available across the country. Sushi became a popular street food that travellers enjoyed in Ryokans or inns that were like rest stops for tired travellers. These days, Americans eat a lot of sushi. There are over 4000 sushi restaurants in the country. In fact, people are developing an interest in sushi in metro cities in India as well.

A. Complete the sentences with correct words from the passage.

1. The ________________ is a very popular street food in Vietnam.
2. The ________________ is the most popular food in the world.
3. Pizza is garnished with ________________.
4. The Turkish doner kebab is made of ________________ bread.
5. Sushi is a bite-sized piece of ________________.
6. Ryokans or inns were like ________________.

B. Briefly answer the following questions.

1. Who brought the pizza to the USA?

____

2. Which are the two best-known types of Italian pizza?

____

3. What is a doner kebab filled with?

____

4. How is sushi served?

____

5. Why is a lot of seafood available in Japan?

____

Way with Words

A. Match the rhyming words.

A	B
1. lump	a. higher
2. fire	b. away
3. bread	c. plump
4. play	d. tin
5. roar	e. fed
6. in	f. door

PREFIX

A **prefix** is a letter or a group of letters added to the beginning of a word.

B. Form the opposites of the following words using prefixes given in the box.

un-	im-	in-	ir-	il-

1. happy: ________________ 6. responsible: ________________

2. possible: ____________

3. even: ____________

4. legible: ____________

5. correct: ____________

7. kind: ____________

8. logical: ____________

9. bearable: ____________

10. polite: ____________

Grammar in Use

Simple Present Tense and Present Continuous Tense

The **simple present tense** is used to talk about facts and habits.
The **present continuous tense** is used to talk about an action taking place at the time of speaking.

A. Fill in the blanks with the present continuous tense of the given verbs.

1. Ravi ____________ *Harry Potter and the Goblet of Fire*. (read)
2. The children ____________ cricket in the park. (play)
3. I ____________ to the museum with my friends. (go)
4. The boy ____________ a letter to his father. (write)
5. The soldiers ____________ towards the village. (march)
6. The little girl ____________ a glass of milk. (drink)
7. My classmates ____________ the national anthem. (sing)
8. I ____________ a film with my parents. (watch)

B. Complete the sentences with the correct form of the verbs given in brackets.

1. The children ____________ right now. (study)
2. Maya always ____________ her hands and feet before sleeping. (wash)
3. Siya usually ____________ black shoes to school. (wear)
4. My sister ____________ a scarf today as she has a holiday. (knit)
5. I think someone ____________ in the park. (shout)
6. My mother ____________ for a morning walk every day. (go)

C. Make sentences with these verbs according to the instructions. One is done for you.

1. pay (*Use present continuous tense*): *The lady is paying the shopkeeper for the bread and eggs.*
2. read (Use simple present tense): ____________
3. visit (Use simple present tense): ____________
4. play (Use *present continuous* tense): ____________
5. run (Use simple present tense): ____________

6. drive (Use *present continuous* tense): ______________________________

7. shop (Use *present continuous* tense): ______________________________

8. sing (Use simple present tense): ______________________________

Listening and Speaking

Listen to a passage. Then, complete the paragraph using information from the passage.

The washerman's donkey was called ________________ . He used to carry ________________ during the day but at night he was free to eat ________________ in a nearby field. Instead of grazing, he would creep into a ________________ and eat vegetables ________________. One night, he met a ________________ and they became ________________. While the donkey ate vegetables, the ________________ ate the ________________ on the farm. They would return to their homes by ________________.

Pen it Down

Write a paragraph about your favourite food item.

You may include these points:

- name of the food item
- place of origin
- where you tasted it first
- which ingredients are used to make it
- why it is your favourite food item
- what it tastes like

Draw or paste a picture of the food item here.

6

Rainmaking

Way with Words

Analogies

A. Choose the word that best completes these analogies. One is done for you.

1. *car is to road as boat is to* ___*water*___
   a. air
   b. land
   c. water
2. a puppy is to a dog as a kitten is to a ____________
   a. cat
   b. lion
   c. bear
3. sun is to day as moon is to ____________
   a. afternoon
   b. night
   c. morning
4. an elbow is to the arm as a knee is to the ____________
   a. head
   b. piano
   c. leg
5. an apple is to fruit as a cabbage is to ____________
   a. vegetable
   b. pulse
   c. salad
6. less is to more as dry is to ____________
   a. winter
   b. summer
   c. wet

B. Use the compound words from the help box to complete the sentences.

fireplace	earthquake	chairperson	headache	bookmark

1. The building was destroyed when an _________________ shook the city.
2. Megha made a wonderful _________________ with handmade paper.
3. The dog was sleeping near the _________________ as it was feeling cold.
4. The _________________ of the company conducted the meeting.
5. Raju was resting as he had a terrible _________________.

Grammar in Use

Adjectives: Degrees of Comparison

Adjectives are words that are used to describe nouns. Adjectives can be in the positive, comparative or superlative form.

A **positive** adjective is the adjective in its basic form.

Example: Sukhdev is a **happy** child.

Comparative adjectives are used when we compare two things or persons.

The comparative degree may be formed by adding **-er** to the adjective, in some cases, and by adding **more** before the adjective, in others.

Examples: Dara is a **happier** child than Sukhdev.
This sofa is **more comfortable** than that one.

Superlative adjectives are used to show that something or someone is the best or worst when compared to all others.

The superlative degree may be formed by adding **-est** to the adjective, in some cases, and by adding **most** before the adjective, in others.

Examples: Joe is the **happiest** child in the class.
This sofa is the **most comfortable**.

A. Write the suitable form of the adjectives given in brackets and complete the sentences.

1. My grandfather is the _________________ person in our house. (elder)
2. I think Rachel is the _________________ dancer in the world. (worse)
3. Deepika is _________________ than Saina at tennis. (good)

4. Our class is ____________ than your class. (disciplined)
5. Aarav has ____________ (few) marbles than Karan, but I have the ____________. (few)
6. My shoes are ____________ than my sister's. (new)
7. This is the ____________ film I have seen till now. (good)
8. The batting line-up of the opposition team is ____________ than ours. (strong)
9. I find the rose ____________ than the lily. (beautiful)

Word Forms: Verbs and Nouns

B. Make sentences with these words, using each as a noun and as a verb.

1. watch (noun): ____________
   watch (verb): ____________
2. play (noun): ____________
   play (verb): ____________
3. rain (noun): ____________
   rain (verb): ____________
4. act (noun): ____________
   act (verb): ____________

Listening and Speaking

Listen to Rohit talk about what he does to make his parents proud. Then, tell your class what you would do to make your parents proud.

You may talk about the following things:

- something you would do at home/in school
- which value/quality will get highlighted through the act
- what your parents' reaction will be

Pen it Down

Imagine that you are Raja. Write a note to your parents to apologize for your bad behaviour during your visit to your grandparents' home.

You can use the following points to write the note:

- mention what you did and why it was wrong

- explain what made you do it
- describe what effect it had on your grandparents
- apologize and promise never to repeat such behaviour

Dear Mother and Father,

7 The Recycling Rap

Way with Words

A. Match the words that are generally used together.

A	B
1. sweet and	a. butter
2. pen and	b. saucer
3. spoon and	c. sour
4. cup and	d. key
5. bread and	e. water
6. lock and	f. paper
7. soap and	g. fork

Names of Cities

B. Find names of these cities in the grid below.

Paris	London	Chennai	Kolkata
Pune	Mumbai	Imphal	Colombo

M	W	P	U	N	E	D	Q	C	P	D	O	P
U	X	H	K	Z	B	E	P	O	A	E	G	Q
M	K	O	L	K	A	T	A	L	R	F	E	R
B	Y	G	M	Y	N	F	O	O	I	G	N	S
A	Z	F	N	X	G	H	N	M	S	H	E	T
I	M	P	H	A	L	I	M	B	C	I	V	U
D	A	D	P	L	O	N	D	O	N	J	A	V
F	N	C	Q	V	K	G	L	Z	B	K	N	W
N	I	B	C	H	E	N	N	A	I	G	H	J

Grammar in Use

Possessive Adjectives and Pronouns

A **possessive adjective** is used before a noun to show its ownership.
Example: That is **her** car.

A **possessive pronoun** is used in place of a noun to show who owns something.
Example: That car is **hers**.

A. Complete the sentences with suitable possessive adjectives or pronouns.

1. That bicycle is ______________. (mine/my)
2. ______________ mother is reading a magazine. (My/Mine)
3. There are so many cars here. I don't know which one is ______________. (ours/our)
4. Ravi left ______________ bag on the shelf. (his/my)
5. This is ______________ dress; that dress is ______________. (my/mine; your/yours)
6. This is ______________ bag, and that bottle is also ______________. (theirs/their)

Main and Auxiliary Verb

A **main verb** is the verb that describes the action in a sentence.

A word that helps the main verb to form the correct tense is called an **auxiliary verb** or a helping verb.

B. Complete the sentences with the correct verbs.

1. The teacher ______________ a book. (is reading/have read)
2. I ______________ playing the piano now. (plays/am playing)
3. They ______________ lemonade outside the school gate. (are selling/has sold)
4. He ______________ his assignments regularly. (do/does)
5. The man ______________ his dinner. (has eaten/have eaten)
6. We ______________ a play last evening. (am watching/were watching)

Listening and Speaking

Listen to the passage and answer the questions that follow.

1. Where did the royal elephant reside?

____

2. Why was he treated well?

____

3. Where did the dog live? Mention two adjectives to describe him.

____

4. Why did the dog sneak into the elephant's shed?

____

5. When did the elephant notice the dog?

____

6. What was the elephant's initial reaction after seeing the dog?

____

7. How did the dog and the elephant become friends?

____

Pen it Down

Your school is organizing a cleanliness drive in the park behind the school. All the students of Class 4 will be taken to the park and given garbage bags, which they will have to fill up. Everyone will receive a certificate from school and the student who fills up the maximum number of garbage bags will be awarded a medal and a book. Write a notice informing the students about this drive.

Remember to include the following details:

- date and time of the event
- the venue
- any prizes or certificates to be given to the participants

8 A Crow in the House

Comprehension

Read the passage and answer the questions.

The next morning, although I had gone to bed so late the night before, I was up frightfully early. The first sparrows were just beginning to chirp sleepily on the slates outside my attic window, when I jumped out of bed and scrambled into my clothes. I could hardly wait to get back to the little house with the big garden – to see the Doctor and his private zoo. For the first time in my life, I forgot all about breakfast; and creeping down the stairs on tiptoe, so as not to wake my mother and father, I opened the front door and popped out into the empty, silent street. When I got to the Doctor's gate, I suddenly thought that perhaps it was too early to call on any one and I began to wonder if the Doctor would be up yet. I looked into the garden. No one seemed to be about. So I opened the gate quietly and went inside. As I turned to the left to go down a path between some hedges, I heard a voice quite close to me say, 'Good morning. How early you are!'

I turned around, and there, sitting on the top of a privet hedge, was the gray parrot, Polynesia. 'Good morning,' I said. 'I suppose I am rather early. Is the Doctor still in bed?' 'Oh no,' said Polynesia. 'He has been up an hour and a half. You'll find him in the house somewhere. The front door is open. Just push it and go in. He is sure to be in the kitchen cooking breakfast – or working in his study. Walk right in. I am waiting to see the sun rise. But upon my word, I believe it's forgotten to rise. Well, don't let me keep you. Run along and see the Doctor.' 'Thank you,' I said. 'I'll go and look for him.' When I opened the front door I could smell meat frying, so I made my way to the kitchen. There I discovered a large kettle boiling away over the fire and some meat and eggs in a dish upon the hearth. It seemed to me that the meat was getting all dried up with the heat. So I pulled the dish a little further away from the fire and went on through the house, looking for the Doctor. I found him at last in the study.

1. What did the narrator do as soon as he woke up?

   ____

2. Why did he creep down the stairs on tiptoe?

   ____

3. What thought struck him when he reached the Doctor's house?

   ____

4. Who was the first one to greet the narrator?

____

5. What did the narrator see on entering the kitchen?

____

6. Where did the narrator find the Doctor?

____

7. Explain the phrase 'frightfully early'.

____

8. Given below are some words from the passage. Look up the dictionary and find their meanings.

   a. attic __________________

   b. scrambled __________________

   c. privet hedge __________________

   d. hearth __________________

Way with Words

WORDS RELATED TO NATURE

Give one word for the following:

1. this is planted in the soil – s _ _ d
2. another other term used for cutting of trees – f _ _ _ _ _ g
3. Large, flying insect – c _ _ _ _ _ t
4. fluffy mass floating in the air – c _ _ _ d
5. a long-tailed songbird – c _ _ _ _ o
6. one gathers these on the beach – s _ _ _ _s

Grammar in Use

USING *WHO* AND *WHICH*

You can use **who** and **which** to join sentences.
Who is used to talk about people and **which** is used to talk about things.

A. Join the following sentences using who or which.

1. The student created a model. She was praised by the judges.

____

2. The bouquet of flowers was delivered to my house. My friend sent it.

____

3. This is the harmonium. It belongs to my mother.

____

4. Bring me the vase. The vase is on the shelf.

____

5. The giant lived in a huge castle. He was strong and cruel.

____

6. I have a cousin. She lives in Pune.

____

SUBJECT-VERB AGREEMENT

When two singular subjects are joined by **and** and they refer to the same person, idea or object, the verb is singular.

Example: Time and tide waits for none.

However, if they refer to two different persons, ideas or things, then the verb is plural.

Example: The poet and the author have arrived.

When two subjects are joined by **or**, **either…or**, or **neither….nor**, the verb agrees with the second subject.

Example: Either Ravi or Naresh is to blame.

When two subjects are joined by **as well as**, **along with**, or **with**, the verb agrees with the first subject.

Example: The teacher, along with the students, is going to the museum.

B. Complete the sentences with was or were.

1. They __________ at the club last evening.
2. It __________ very humid yesterday.
3. There __________ many bottles of fruit juice on the table.
4. There __________ two puppies in the kennel.
5. Only one piece of chocolate __________ left for me.
6. I __________ playing video games last evening.

Listening and Speaking

What do we say when someone asks us to do something and we are not able to do it?

Here are some common expressions we use to refuse.

1. I am sorry but I can't...
2. I don't want to...
3. I'd better not...
4. No, but thanks for asking.

Use suitable expressions to refuse in the following situations.

1. Would you like some cake?
2. Shall we go for a picnic on Sunday?
3. Would you mind helping me?
4. Would you like to join us for lunch?

Pen it Down

Look at the pictures carefully and describe the picnic.

You may include the following points:

- location of the picnic spot
- time of the year
- who went for the picnic
- fun activities and food

9 Life Cycle of a Butterfly

Way with Words

Jumbled Words and Sentences

A. Read the following clues and guess the words.

1. bonbacek ____________ (insects do not have this)
2. atannene ____________ (insects have this on their head)
3. datorpres ____________ (those who hunt other animals)
4. siteparas ____________ (those who live and feed on other animals)
5. cktecri ____________ (insect with the same name as a sport)
6. adcica ____________ (loudest insects among all)

B. Rearrange the following words to form meaningful sentences. Punctuate the sentences accordingly.

1. jumped/the/over/fence/horse/the

____

2. on/the/a/chewing/was/bone/dog

____

3. the/holes/in/woodpecker/trees/makes/the/trunks/of

____

4. the/was/horse/his/farmer/brown/riding

____

5. beautiful/spreads/the/wings/its/peacock

____

6. the/in/kitten/the/basket/was/lying

____

Grammar in Use

SIMPLE FUTURE TENSE: USING 'WILL'

The Simple future tense is used to talk about events that will take place in the future. We use **will** or **shall** before the main verb to form the simple future tense.

A. Complete the sentences with the future form of the verbs in the box.

ask	switch off	turn off	water	throw	plant

1. I ____________ the plants in my house.
2. I ____________ more trees.
3. I ____________ the waste in the bin.
4. I ____________ the tap when I brush my teeth.
5. I ____________ the lights when they are not in use.
6. I ____________ my friends to do so too.

B. Use the correct future form of the verbs and complete the paragraph.

read	return	bake	drive	visit	pluck	go	play

Tomorrow, I ____________ my grandparents. We ____________ by our car. My dad ____________ us to my grandparents' house. My grandmother ____________ a cake for me. I ____________ lots of games with my grandfather. I ____________ fresh oranges from the trees in their garden and catch butterflies. After lunch, grandfather ____________ my favourite story to me. We ____________ in the evening.

Listening and Speaking

Listen to the poem 'On the Grasshopper and Cricket' by John Keats twice. In pairs, recite the poem again with correct intonation and stress.

When you recite a poem, remember the following points:

- Try to understand the meaning of the poem.
- Stress on the correct words to express the meaning.
- Remember that voice modulation is very important.
- Ensure that your facial expressions and gestures match the subject and tone of the poem.

Pen it Down

Imagine that you are a member of the Science Club of your school and you have been asked to write an article for the club's monthly magazine. In one paragraph, describe the life cycle of a butterfly. Draw a diagram to show the various stages of its life cycle.

Test Paper

Comprehension

Read the poem 'Roads' by Rachel Field and answer the questions that follow.

A road might lead to anywhere —
To harbour towns and quays,

Or to a witch's pointed house
Hidden by bristly trees.

It might lead past the tailor's door,
Where he sews with needle and thread,

Or by Miss Pirn the milliner's,
With her hats for every head.

It might be a road to a great, dark cave
With treasure and gold piled high,

Or a road with a mountain tied to its end,
Bluchumped against the sky.

Oh, a road might lead you anywhere —
To Mexico or Maine.

But then, it might just fool you, and —
Lead you back home again!

1. What is hidden by the trees?

   ____

2. What is the tailor doing?

   ____

3. What will one find in Miss Pirn's shop?

   ____

4. Where will you find treasure?

____

5. How does the road fool you?

____

6. Which city has been mentioned in the poem?

____

7. Mention any two adjectives used in the poem.

____

8. Given below are some words from the poem. Look up a dictionary and find their meanings.

   a. quays _______________ b. bristly _______________

   c. milliner _______________ d. harbour _______________

Way with Words

A. Write a rhyming word for each of the given words.

1. house _______________
2. thread _______________
3. cave _______________
4. head _______________
5. end _______________

B. Make sentences with the following words.

1. witch _______________
2. cave _______________
3. sews _______________
4. mountain _______________
5. lead _______________

C. Rearrange the following words to make meaningful sentences. Punctuate the sentences accordingly.

1. juicy/gave/a/puppy/rohan/his/bone/to

   ____

2. you/news/have/the/sad/heard

   ____

3. a/was/dance/it/wonderful/what/programme

   ____

4. the/from/get/lamp/room/table/the

____

5. tears/the/of/in/teacher's/there/eyes/were/joy

____

D. Add a suitable word to each of these words to form compound words.

1. battle ______________
2. book ______________
3. gentle ______________
4. house ______________
5. head ______________
6. rain ______________
7. pen ______________
8. sea ______________
9. beach ______________
10. bed ______________

E. Write a suitable name to describe each set of word. One is done for you.

1. *bed, table, sofa: furniture*
2. pen, pencil, eraser: ______________
3. pineapple, custard apple, melon: ______________
4. cuckoo, parrot, peacock: ______________
5. north, south, east: ______________
6. cricket, football, hockey: ______________
7. January, April, August: ______________

Grammar in Use

A. Complete the sentences with suitable articles.

1. My sister wants to be ________ pilot.
2. The girls clean ________ room once ________ week.
3. I read ________ interesting article in ________ newspaper.
4. Meg bought ________ chocolate for her brother.
5. Smita wrote ________ letter to ________ warden of ________ hostel.

B. Underline the verbs in these sentences and identify their tense.

1. Sumit is buying a laptop for his younger brother. ______________
2. Raj drank five glasses of mango juice yesterday. ______________
3. We will be meeting our friends next month. ______________
4. My grandfather reads the newspaper every morning. ______________
5. The children were sailing paper boats in the puddles. ______________
6. The cat was waiting for the mouse to come out of its hole. ______________

C. Write suitable adjectives for each noun. The first letter of the adjective has been given.

1. l ________ hair		5. d ________ food	
2. b ________ story		6. s ________ boy	
3. p ________ climate		7. w ________ clothes	
4. c ________ bus		8. h ________ storm	

D. Identify the subject and predicate in the following sentences and write them in the appropriate columns.

1. The hunter caught the deer.
2. There are many fruit trees in the garden.
3. The naughty boy came late to the class.
4. My mother baked a chocolate cake for me.
5. The setting sun looked beautiful.

	SUBJECT	PREDICATE
1.		
2.		
3.		
4.		
5.		

Listening and Speaking

Imagine that you have gone to a new place and cannot find the way to your hotel. Form pairs and have a conversation with your partner, asking him/her for help.

Pen it Down

A. Imagine that your pet can talk. What do you think it would tell you? How would you react to such a situation? Write the conversation you would have with your pet.

____

____

B. Write a letter to your friend, thanking her for the book she gifted you on your birthday.

10

Oliver Goes to London

Way with Words

Synonyms

A. Match the words with their synonyms.

A	B
1. meadow	a. completed
2. weak	b. noisy
3. damp	c. hard
4. strange	d. feeble
5. tired	e. unusual
6. finished	f. moist
7. loud	g. just
8. difficult	h. exhausted
9. fair	i. pasture

Suffixes: *-ind* and *ild*

B. Complete the words with -ind or -ild.

1. Fatima helped the bl_______ woman cross the road.
2. Please f_______ my water bottle.
3. Ravi was asked to m_______ the class.
4. There are many w_______ animals in the circus.
5. The day was sunny and m_______, perfect for a picnic.
6. My uncle had to gr_______ the wheat to make flour.
7. The donkey kicked the thief with its h_______ legs.
8. The naughty ch_______ has broken the vase.
9. We are going to bu_______ a castle using sand.
10. I need a rope to b_______ these books together.

Grammar in Use

Prepositions

A **preposition** is a word that is generally placed before a noun or a pronoun to refer to its relation with some other word in the sentence. It tells us about position and time.

A. Complete the sentences with for, since, at or in.

1. I have been waiting for Sunny ______ four hours.
2. My aunt has been living in Germany ______ 2007.
3. I will meet you ______ the bus stop.
4. Is your house ______ the village?
5. My grandfather gifted me a pen ______ my birthday.
6. We must not be late ______ school.
7. My uncle is ______ Lucknow now.
8. We haven't been on a holiday ______ January.

B. Complete the sentences with suitable prepositions.

1. The postman is knocking __________ the door.
2. I usually go for a walk __________ the evening.
3. Alice was lying __________ the grass.
4. The lion pounced __________ its prey.
5. The boy jumped __________ the fence.
6. He stayed __________ the hotel __________ two weeks.
7. Distribute the sweets __________ your classmates.
8. The villagers built a bridge __________ the river.

Transitive and Intransitive Verbs

A **transitive verb** is a verb that needs an object to receive the action.
An **intransitive verb** is a verb that does not need an object to receive the action.

C. Read each sentence and write T if the underlined verb is transitive and I if the verb is intransitive.

1. The boy <u>threw</u> the ball over the fence. ☐
2. The sun <u>rises</u> in the east. ☐
3. The little girl <u>smiled</u>. ☐
4. Rahul <u>waved</u> at me. ☐
5. The class <u>shouted</u> together. ☐
6. The teacher <u>scolded</u> the class. ☐

D. Make sentences with the following words, first using them as transitive and then as intransitive verbs.

1. *raised*

   transitive ______________________________

   intransitive ______________________________

2. *write*

   transitive ______________________________

   intransitive ______________________________

3. *built*

   transitive ______________________________

   intransitive ______________________________

4. *bought*

   transitive ______________________________

   intransitive ______________________________

5. *sleep*

   transitive ______________________________

   intransitive ______________________________

Listening and Speaking

Listen to a short story. Work in pairs and retell the story without missing out on the main idea and the details. What do you think is the moral of the story? Discuss with your classmates.

Pen it Down

A. Oliver is a young boy who has run away from his adoptive home, hoping to lead a better life in London. Write a character sketch of Oliver supporting it with examples from the story.

You may talk about what the following points:

- why he chose to run away
- his journey to London
- how he overcame his difficulties
- his interaction with the Artful Dodger

____

____

B. **Write a short composition about the Artful Dodger describing what happens to him after the story ends. Complete his story from your imagination.**

11

The Naga Dragon's Lair

Way with Words

SIMILE

A. The following similes have been mixed up. Write them correctly in the space given below.

as smooth as an owl	as cunning as a wolf	as wise as silk
as hungry as a fox	as cool as a bee	as busy as a cucumber
as pretty as coal	as dark as a picture	

1. ______________________
2. ______________________
3. ______________________
4. ______________________
5. ______________________
6. ______________________
7. ______________________
8. ______________________

B. Match the names of objects with their colour.

A	B
1. lemongrass	a. yellow
2. cotton	b. orange
3. potato	c. white
4. carrot	d. green
5. sunflower	e. black
6. coal tar	f. brown

Grammar in Use

Types of Adjectives

You know that adjectives are words which describe a noun or a pronoun.

Adjectives of quality are used to tell the quality of a person or a thing.

Example: **Ferocious** Naga dragons had taken them prisoner.

Adjectives of quantity are used to show the amount of something.

Example: Maung Thu Ka Ta went on **many** adventures.

Adjectives of number are used to tell the number of something.

Example: The king spoke to the **three** courtiers.

Demonstrative adjectives are used to point out a person or a thing in a sentence.

Example: **That** Naga dragon is huge.

A. Complete the sentences with suitable adjectives.

1. There are ________________ apples in the cart. (adjective of number)
2. We had to take a ________________ route to reach the tourist spot. (adjective of quality)
3. ________________ bag is not mine. (demonstrative adjective)
4. Do you have ________________ money to buy a big house? (adjective of quantity)
5. Deliver ________________ parcel to Mrs. Das at once. (demonstrative adjective)
6. He was wearing a ________________ shirt yesterday. (adjective of quality)

Types of Adverbs

An **adverb** is a word that tell us more about a verb.

Adverbs of time tell us when something takes place.

Example: The queen went on the journey **yesterday**.

Adverbs of place tell us where something takes place.

Example: The people were standing **outside** the palace.

Adverbs of manner tell us how or in what manner something takes place.

Example: The new land was lit up **brightly**.

B. Choose suitable adverbs from the box to complete the sentences.

there	everywhere	tomorrow	heavily	fast	loudly

1. Sanjay speaks very ________________.
2. Wait for me ________________.
3. Please return the library book ________________.
4. We looked ________________ for the lost wallet.

5. It snows ________ in Kashmir during winters.

6. The teacher asked us to walk ________.

Listening and Speaking

Listen to the conversation and complete the passage.

Rahul and his mother were going to visit his ________ because she was ________. Rahul did not want to go as he had a ________ at ________. His mother got ________ with him. She was determined to visit her ________ that day but promised that they would return ________. Rahul said that the house was quite ________ and the bus stopped ________. Mother said that they would take a ________ to save time. Rahul was ________ and got ________.

Pen it Down

Your teacher divided the class into groups for a science project. On the day of the project, you realise that your friend has forgotten important documents and is in tears. Write a short, personal account of how you saved your friend from getting into trouble with his/her group members and the teacher.

12
The Sound Collector

Way with Words

A. Write the nouns given in the box beside the sounds made by them.

clouds	drums	wind	crackers	kettles	clocks

1. burst: ____________________
2. whistle: ____________________
3. beat: ____________________
4. tick-tock: ____________________
5. howls: ____________________
6. rumble: ____________________

IMAGERY

Imagery is the use of words in such a way that it appeals to our senses of smell, sight, sound, taste or touch.

Example: Lightning **cracked** across the sky in **jagged, blue lines**.

Here, the word **cracked** refers to the sound of lightning. It is an example of sound imagery.

The words **jagged, blue lines** refers to the way the lightning looks. It is an example of sight imagery.

B. In a sentence, write an imagery of your own according to the directions given and the type of imagery mentioned.

1. sense of smell - ____________________ (a smell related to Nature)
2. sense of sight - ____________________ (your favourite holiday spot)
3. sense of sound - ____________________ (a sound that makes you happy)
4. sense of taste - ____________________ (your favourite dish)
5. sense of touch - ____________________ (the touch of an animal, bird or any other non-human creature)

Grammar in Use

Past Continuous Tense

The past continuous tense describes an ongoing action in the past.

Example: The children **were playing** a game of kho-kho in the afternoon.

A. Complete the sentences with the past or present continuous tense of the verbs in the brackets.

1. Jaya ____________ television when her parents came in. (watch)
2. I ____________ the newspaper now. (read)
3. Yesterday at 10.45 pm, Santosh ____________. (sleep)
4. Raman ____________ his homework at the moment. (do)
5. We ____________ our cousins next Sunday. (meet)
6. I could not help my mother as I ____________ for my test. (study)

B. Write the tense of the verbs according to the directions given.

1. I bend: ______________________________ (simple present)
2. It bites: ______________________________ (present continuous)
3. They bring: ______________________________ (past continuous)
4. They pay: ______________________________ (simple past)
5. I build: ______________________________ (past continuous)
6. We lose: ______________________________ (simple future)
7. You catch: ______________________________ (simple past)
8. They find: ______________________________ (simple future)
9. She buys: ______________________________ (past continuous)
10. They fight: ______________________________ (simple present)
11. I dream: ______________________________ (simple future)
12. You think: ______________________________ (simple past)

Write a paragraph about a visit to a local bazar. Describe the sights, sounds and

Listening and Speaking

A. Listen carefully to the various sounds. Identify the sounds and number them in the order in which you hear them.

☐	cry of pain	☐	book dropping with a thud
☐	whimper of a dog	☐	clanging of pots and pans

☐ gurgle of a stream

☐ tinkling of glass

☐ screeching of a crow

☐ tinkle of bells

☐ clatter of plates

B. Which are the sounds that you hear every day? Talk about five such sounds.

Pen it Down

Write a paragraph about a visit to a local bazaar. Describe the sights, sounds and smells that you come across and the things you buy. Use plenty of adjectives to make your description interesting.

13

The Wizard of Oz

Way with Words

Anagrams

An **anagram** is a word that is formed by rearranging the letters of another word.
Example: sale → seal

A. Match the words with their anagrams.

A	B
1. boots	a. pace
2. cape	b. taco
3. aprons	c. boost
4. coat	d. thirst
5. robe	e. parson
6. t-shirt	f. bore

Grammar in Use

Phrase

A **phrase** is a group of words that does not have a verb. A phrase does not make complete sense by itself.
Example: The friends walked **for three days**.

A. Make sentences with these phrases.

1. at the museum

____

2. because of the rain

____

3. during the winter season

4. over the fence

5. at the bus stop

6. before the storm

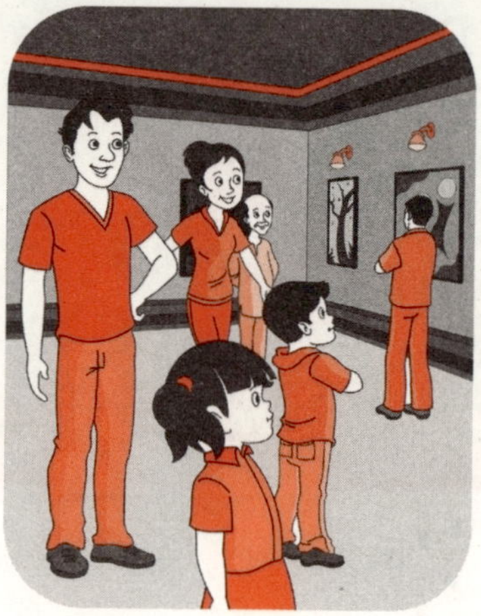

B. Complete the following sentences with suitable phrases.

1. We started planning for the party
2. We went home
3. The boy ate the food
4. We have to stay in class until
5. We should wash our hands
6. We could not return the book

Apostrophe to Show Possession

As **apostrophe** is used to show that something belongs to someone.

C. Write these phrases again, adding apostrophes.

1. the suns rays
2. the birds wings
3. the shops window
4. a boys coat
5. a girls dress

D. Rewrite the following sentences after adding the apostrophes.

1. The mens shoes are kept on a different shelf.
2. The students reports were collected by the teacher.
3. She got an interesting childrens book as a birthday present.
4. The babies toys were lying on the floor.
5. I borrowed Ritus guitar for a day.
6. Today is Taruns birthday.
7. Mohans dog is very friendly and playful.
8. I am going to Natashas house in the evening.

Listening and Speaking

A. Listen carefully to the poem 'General Store' by Rachel Field. Write the words from the poem that rhyme with the following words.

1. store: ____
2. inside: ____
3. everything: ____
4. bright: ____
5. lunches: ____
6. myself: ____
7. say: ____

B. Think of three pairs of rhyming words and say them aloud.

Pen it Down

A play based on *The Wizard of Oz* will be staged on the occasion of your school's Annual Day. Create a poster asking students to attend the event. Your poster should include the following details:

- the venue of the play
- the time when the play would start
- the duration of the play
- the place from where tickets can be bought
- the price of the tickets
- any important highlight, such as the chief guest or star performers.

14

The Lighthouse

Way with Words

Forming New Words

A. Read the clues and add a letter to the given words to make new words.

1. Which letter can be added to **sea** to make it a word meaning 'something to sit on'?
   sea__
2. Which letter can be added to **men** to make it a word meaning 'unkind'?
   me__n
3. Which letter can be added to **star** to make it a word meaning 'to look at something
   continuously'?
   star__
4. Which letter can be added to **and** to make it a word meaning 'a part of the body'?
   __and
5. Which letter can be added to **mall** to make it a word meaning 'of a size that is less than normal'?
   __mall
6. Which letter can be added to **send** to make it a word meaning 'to pay for something'?
   s__end

B. Change one letter in each word to make a new word.

1. shore: sh__re
2. night: __ight
3. lonely: lo__ely
4. trim: __rim
5. ship: s__ip
6. grip: __rip
7. feet: fee__
8. wake: __ake
9. bare: bar__
10. know: now
11. note: ote
12. hoop: hoo__

Grammar in Use

PARTICIPLES: PRESENT AND PAST

A **present participle** is formed by adding **-ing** to the base form of a regular verb. It can serve as a verb in continuous tense or as an adjective.

Example: Men lived to guard that **moving** light,

A **past participle** is used to show a completed action. It ends in **-ed**, **-d**, **it**, **-en** or **-n**. It can be used as an adjective as well.

Example: The painting of the lighthouse was done on **stretched** canvas.

A. Complete the sentences with the past participle form of the verbs in the brackets.

1. I have never ________________ how you helped me. (forget)
2. The teacher had ________________ Maya leaving the room quietly. (catch)
3. Have you ________________ my new watch? (see)
4. Walk slowly! Someone has ________________ oil on the floor. (drop)
5. Ruskin Bond has ________________ wonderful stories for children. (write)
6. Have you ________________ my pencil box? (see)

B. Read the following sentences and underline the present or past participles.

1. The walk to the park was very tiring.
2. Everyone was bored at his show.
3. He scared the little girl by telling her ghost stories.
4. She ran in a hurry as the dog was chasing her.
5. He was very pleased with his results and kept smiling the entire day.

A. Read the following words aloud and underline the silent letters. One is done for you.

Listening and Speaking

1. *debt*	5. subtle	7. calf
3. sign	9. island	11. castle
2. muscle	6. knock	8. column
4. hour	10. honest	12. watch

B. You have just returned from a vacation in a seaside town/village. Work in pairs and prepare a short role-play telling your partner about your experience.

You may include the following points in your conversation:

- location of the place
- weather and climate
- local people and cuisine
- tourist spots
- differences between the seaside and where you live
- feelings, emotions and memorable moments

Pen it Down

Imagine that your school has planned a trip to a lighthouse located in a seaside town nearby. Create an invitation card on behalf of the school inviting the students and teachers to the event.

You may talk about the following things:

- date, time and location of the event
- safety measures to be followed during the visit
- a line about the history, role of the lighthouse in the past, and its current significance in the town's history

15 How the Leopard Got His Spots

Way with Words

A. Find the names of these animals in the word grid.

leopard giraffe zebra elephant cheetah baboon dog tiger

L	E	L	E	P	H	A	N	T
E	A	S	D	F	H	J	G	H
O	E	C	H	E	E	T	A	H
P	D	W	Q	T	H	H	G	H
A	O	T	D	I	G	B	F	D
R	G	G	S	G	I	A	I	X
D	R	Y	A	E	R	B	Y	V
U	Z	E	B	R	A	O	T	X
U	F	F	G	J	F	O	R	D
J	S	Y	U	P	F	N	O	F
M	B	X	Z	A	E	A	S	E

Suffixes

B. Add the suffixes -ness, -ly, -ful, -able or -ment to the words in the brackets and complete the sentences using the words.

1. We all finished our work ____________ (proper).
2. We ____________ (usual) visit our grandparents in holidays.
3. Are you ____________ (comfort) in this chair?
4. The puppies played ____________ (happy) with the cats.
5. What a ____________ (beauty) painting!

6. I have tried to show an ________________ (improve) in my work.
7. Mrs Gupta showed a lot of ________________ (kind) towards the poor boy.
8. The show was a good source of ________________ (entertain) for the audience.
9. She found the new book ________________ (enjoy).
10. We have seen tremendous scientific ________________ (advance) in the last decade.

Abbreviations

C. Choose the correct full forms of the given abbreviations.

United Nations	Example	British Broadcasting Corporation
Short Message Service	Doctor	Number

1. E.g.: ________________
2. No.: ________________
3. UN: ________________
4. BBC: ________________
5. SMS: ________________
6. Dr: ________________

Grammar in Use

Adjective Phrase

A group of words that acts as an adjective in a sentence is called an **adjective phrase**.
Examples: made of wood, a lady of courage, without sleep

A. Replace each adjective with an adjective phrase. One is done for you.

1. He was a **famous** scientist.
   He was a scientist <u>of great fame</u>.
2. This bag is **useless** to us.
   ____
3. A **valuable** photograph was found in the attic.
   ____
4. The sage lived in a **mud** hut.
   ____
5. He was a **fearless** ruler.
   ____

B. Complete the sentences with the correct options.

1. I have ______________________ phone.
   a. a mobile expensive b. an expensive mobile
2. The ______________________ guests were from Germany.
   a. first four b. four first
3. My mother has ______________________ hair.
   a. black long b. long black
4. My friend bought a ______________________ car.
   a. red fast b. fast red
5. Raj bought ______________________ knife for his best friend.
   a. a Swiss army b. an army Swiss
6. My uncle has a ______________________ jacket.
   a. brown leather b. leather brown
7. Our team has a number of ______________________.
   a. skilful players b. players skilful
8. We were amazed by the ______________________.
   a. events extraordinary b. extraordinary events

Listening and Speaking

Listen to the story carefully and put the following events in the correct order.

The leopard saw the empty drum. ☐

The leopard got very angry. ☐

The jackal was wandering in search of food. ☐

The jackal beat the drum with his front paws. ☐

The jackal told the leopard there was an animal inside the drum. ☐

The leopard was attracted by the sound of the drum. ☐

The jackal found a drum in the battle field. ☐

The leopard pounced on the jackal and killed him. ☐

Pen it Down

Your family wants to go to the national park in Ranthambore in Rajasthan for your next vacation. Ranthambore is known for its Tiger Safari. Research the topic and write a paragraph about the place and how best to spend your vacation there.

You can include the following points:

- the top 5 things to visit or see there
- the best route to get there, mode of travel and time of year to go there
- which animals and birds can be viewed there
- other local sights and highlights that should not be missed

16

The Girl Who Stepped on the Loaf

Way with Words

MAGICAL CREATURES

A. You learnt about the elf, a magical creature, in the play. Now match the names of these magical creatures with their correct pictures..

Magical creature	Image
1. fairy	a. 
2. witch	b. 
3. dragon	c. 
4. wizard	d. 
5. griffin	e. 
6. unicorn	f. 

B. Find the antonyms of these words in the word grid.

greedy enemy destroy blunt present private failure rough

B	F	C	D	E	F	G	A	G	I	U
C	R	E	A	T	E	F	G	H	I	J
N	I	O	P	Q	R	S	T	U	V	W
A	E	B	G	S	U	C	C	E	S	S
F	N	G	E	M	M	N	O	P	Q	H
U	D	V	N	O	W	X	Y	Z	B	A
C	D	F	E	O	G	E	H	I	J	R
N	O	P	R	T	Q	R	S	T	U	P
Y	Z	A	O	H	B	C	D	E	F	G
K	L	M	U	P	U	B	L	I	C	L
R	A	B	S	E	N	T	X	Y	Z	A

C. Solve the crossword puzzle with the plural form of each noun.

Across:

5. tomato
2. child
6. sheep
7. leaf

Down:

1. glass
2. city
3. elf
4. shelf

Grammar in Use

DIRECT AND INDIRECT SPEECH

Read these sentences.

My mother said, 'I am going to the office.'

My mother said that she was going to the office.

The first sentence is in **direct speech** as it uses the actual words of the speaker.

The second sentence is in **indirect speech** as it reports what the speaker said.

Remember the following rules when you change a sentence in direct speech to indirect speech:

- first and second person pronouns (*I, we, you*) in direct speech change to 3rd person pronoun (*he, she, they*) in indirect speech.

Example: Naman said, 'I live in Mumbai.' Naman said that he lives in Mumbai.

- Present tense in direct speech changes to past tense in indirect speech.

Example: Maya said, 'Rohit plays cricket.' Maya said that Rohit played cricket.

- Inverted commas are used only in direct speech.

Example: Aman said, 'I don't like junk food.' Aman said that he didn't like junk food.

- If the direct speech expresses a habit or a universal truth, the tense of the verb in direct speech does not change.

Example: Sia said, 'I go for a walk every morning.' Sia said that she goes for a walk every morning.

A. Change these sentences from direct to indirect speech. One is done for you.

1. Arin said, 'I am writing a letter now.'
   Arin said that he was writing a letter then.
2. The teacher says, 'The Earth rotates on its axis.'
   ____
3. The boy said, 'I will watch the match tomorrow.'
   ____
4. Rahul said to me, 'I have completed my work.'
   ____

5. The policeman said to John, 'Where do you live?'
   ____
6. I said, 'I bought a new bag yesterday.'
   ____
7. Mummy said to me, 'Clean up your room.'
   ____

Error Correction

B. Rewrite the sentences after correcting the errors. One is done for you.

1. My sister is young than me.
   My sister is younger than me.
2. He plays the guitar well, don't he?
3. My father work in a bank since 2011.
4. Faisal jumped onto the pond for a swim.
5. Debesh and Agni was playing chess.
6. I had sandwich for breakfast.
7. The cat climbed in the tree.

Listening and Speaking

Read the situations below and in pairs, role-play any two scenarios and talk about what you should do in each situation. Ensure that both your partner and you have an equal number of dialogues.

- I trained for the singing competition but I missed the audition.
- I bought an ice cream and came home before I realised that it wasn't the flavour I had paid for.
- I bought a video game, but when I came home I found that it was defective.
- I need to find some information for my history project but my computer is not working.

Pen it Down

Write a one-act play about a fairy, an elf and a child, with dialogues for each character. Remember that a one-act play is different from a story. Some of the features of a one-act play are:

- there is generally a single setting
- usually one important event is highlighted
- there are no breaks in the plot or action
- the dialogues are precise and to the point
- there are fewer characters

You can include the following points:

- where did all of them meet
- what kind of a fairy was she
- was the elf good or bad
- did they use their magical powers
- did they help the child or cause him harm
- were the fairy and elf friends or enemies

Humour

17

My Elephant is Missing

Way with Words

A. Match each object with the place where it is found.

Object	Place
1. mattress	a. library
2. mouthwash	b. kitchen
3. bookshelf	c. factory
4. tongs	d. bedroom
5. machinery	e. office
6. files	f. washroom

Homonyms

The word 'trunk' refers to a heavy box or a container. It also means the main woody stem of a tree. It is a homonym.

B. Find five more homonyms from the dictionary and make sentences with them to bring out the difference in their meanings.

1. ____________________

____

2. ____________________

____

3. ____________________

____

4. ____________________

____

5. ____________________

____

Grammar in Use

Apostrophe for Contractions

Contractions are shortened forms of words where the missing letter is replaced by an apostrophe.

A. Complete the sentences using the correct options.

1. ______________ you like to get good marks in history?
   a. Wouldn't b. Would'nt
2. He ______________ make it to the meeting.
   a. can'not b. can't
3. ______________ conduct the dance classes on Sunday.
   a. We'll b. Wel'l
4. ______________ planning a surprise party for their parents.
   a. Theyr'e b. They're
5. ______________ collected a lot of money for the old age home.
   a. They'd b. They'ad
6. ______________ the book I was looking for.
   a. That's b. Thats'

B. Write the correct short form of the following words in the given space.

1. do not: ______________
2. must not: ______________
3. should not: ______________
4. has not: ______________
5. is not: ______________
6. are not: ______________

Listening and Speaking

Listen and repeat these words aloud. Identify the words with the soft 'th' sound as in 'think', and the hard 'th' sound as in 'that'. Write them in the correct columns.

these thick thumb together them month though thin

Soft th	Hard th

Pen it Down

You have noticed that some children in your society ill-treat the animals that roam around in the neighbourhood. As the secretary of the Youth Club, you decide to put up a notice on the society gate about ending cruelty towards animals and raising awareness about the need to be kind to them.

- inform the children about the fact that animals also feel pain
- instil in them the desire to take care of the street animals
- remind all about the consequences – punishments and fines

18

Harriet and the Underground Railroad

Comprehension

Read the passage and answer the questions.

Ellis Island is a historical site, a short distance away from the symbol of America, the Statue of Liberty, on Liberty Island. Ellis Island is located at the mouth of the Hudson river between New York and New Jersey. From 1892, for more than 60 years, it served as an immigration station or a place where people coming into the United States were examined to see if they were fit to enter the country. However, in 1954 it was closed down. It saw the arrival of millions of immigrants. In fact, it was calculated that nearly 40 per cent of all US citizens has at least one ancestor who came through Ellis Island.

Ellis Island was opened to manage the millions of people who fled Europe to find better opportunities in America. They left their homes because of war, drought, famine hoping to escape these difficulties in the New World. After a dangerous journey by sea, the immigrants who arrived on the island waited in long queues for medical and legal checks to find out if they were fit to enter the United States. If they were ill, they were quarantined on the island, so that these diseases could not infect others. If they got better in a certain period, they were allowed into the country. If not, they were sent back. Some even died there.

Doctors checked the immigrants for more than 60 diseases and disabilities. Those who were suspected of having a disease or disability were made to stay on for a more thorough check-up. All the immigrants were checked very carefully for trachoma, an infectious eye condition. Trachoma was the cause of people being sent away more than any other illness.

In 1917, Ellis Island served as a hospital for the US Army, a station for members of the Navy and as a place to hold people who were not supposed to be in the USA. By 1918, the Army took over Ellis Island and created a temporary way station to take care of the sick and wounded American soldiers. The Immigrant Quota Act of 1921 and the National Origins Act of 1924 greatly reduced the number and nationality of immigrants allowed into the United States. This put an end to the era of mass immigration into New York. After this, a smaller number of immigrants came through Ellis Island, where they were held back for a short period of time.

Ellis Island became a tourist spot for the first time in 1976. People can now tour the Ellis Island Museum of Immigration in the restored Main Arrivals Hall and find their ancestors by going through the immigrant arrival records.

A. Fill in the blanks with suitable words.

1. Ellis Island is a ____________ site.
2. People made a dangerous _______ by sea to arrive on Ellis Island.
3. __________ was an infectious eye condition.
4. In 1917, Ellis Island served as a __________ for the US army.
5. Ellis Island became a _________ spot for the first time in 1976.

B. State whether the following statements are true or false. Correct the false statements.

1. Ellis Island is located between New York and Chicago.

____

2. The immigrants arrived on Ellis Island by sea.

____

3. Ellis Island was opened to the public in 1976.

____

4. The immigrants who arrived on Ellis Island waited in long queues for food and shelter.

____

C. Answer the following questions.

1. For 60 years, what was Ellis Island used for?

____

____

____

2. Why did the immigrants leave their homes?

____

____

____

3. What happened if they were ill?

____

____

4. Who took over Ellis Island in 1918 and why?

____

____

____

5. What can people now do in the Ellis Island Museum of Immigration?

____

____

____

Way with Words

Idioms with *Head*

A. Match the idioms that use the word 'head' with their meanings.

Idioms	Meanings
1. a cool head	a. an early start on something
2. a head start	b. to prevent something from happening
3. a roof over your head	c. to be in charge of
4. to head for something	d. the ability to stay calm
5. head off	e. a place to live
6. head up	f. to leave for some destination

B. Match the nouns in Column A with the verbs in Column B.

A	B
1. crossword	a. skip
2. vegetables	b. swim
3. rope	c. solve
4. door	d. ring
5. pool	e. cut
6. bell	f. knock

Grammar in Use

Subject–Verb Agreement

A subject and a verb are said to be in agreement when they agree in number. A singular subject should have a singular verb, and a plural subject should have a plural verb.

Example: The **slaves were** glad to receive help from Harriet.

A. Complete the sentences using the correct forms of the verbs.

1. Either my brother or my cousin ________ (is/are) playing video games.
2. Both Lisa and Laila ________ (were/was) present for the meeting.
3. The cost of grapes ________ (has/have) gone up.
4. The teacher along with her students ________ (is/are) going for a picnic.
5. Everyone ________ (have/has) read the book.
6. One of the important files ________ (are/is) missing.

CONJUNCTIONS

You know that conjunctions link other words and phrases together.
The conjunction **as** is used to give reason for an action or event.
Example: I did not go out to play as it was raining.
The conjunction **while** is used to talk about two actions that happen at the same time.
Example: My mother is baking a cake **while** my father is cooking pasta.

B. Complete the sentences with as or while.

1. Please wait ________________ I fill up the form.
2. Please carry an umbrella ________________ it is raining heavily.
3. I ate an ice cream ________________ I was waiting at the stop.
4. Rita did not attend school ________________ she was unwell.
5. ________________ Koyal was absent, she could not attend the music class.
6. He was so tired that he fell asleep ________________ the class was going on.

C. Complete the sentences with suitable conjunctions.

1. My mother welcomed my friends ________________ offered them snacks.
2. You can come with me today ____________ go with her tomorrow to watch the film.
3. My neighbour is not rich ________________ she is generous.
4. My cousin ________________ I go to school together.
5. Ravi is thin ________________ he is quite strong.

Listening and Speaking

Imagine that you are a famous woman personality from India who has contributed to the field of science, literature, social work or politics. You are a role model for students from all over the world. You have been invited by a well-known school to address the children and share your experiences with them.

You may include the following points in your speech:

- some information about your childhood
- people who inspired you
- what changes you would like to bring about in society
- what are the challenges faced by you
- message for the young students

Pen it Down

Write an e-mail to your friend telling him/her the importance of treating people who work for us with respect.

You may use the following ideas to write your e-mail:

- importance of respecting all people
- importance of dignity of labour
- importance of developing a sense of empathy for others
- importance of being sensitive to the needs of others

Assessment

Comprehension

Text A. Read this Jataka tale about a tortoise that loved his earthly home too much. Then answer the questions.

When Brahmadatta was the King of Benaras, the Buddha was reborn as a human child in a potter's family. Close to the great river of Varanasi, was a lake. When there was a lot of water, the river and lake became one; but when the water was low, they were apart. The fish and tortoises knew when it would be rainy and when there would be a drought.

One year there was a drought, so they swam into the river. However, one tortoise would not go into the river, because he felt that since he was born in the lake, he could not leave it. He dug a hole and buried himself, just where the Buddha used to come to collect clay for the pots. One day, the Buddha came to get some clay and he dug down, until he cracked the tortoise's shell, turning him out on the ground as if he were a lump of clay. In pain, the tortoise thought, 'Here I am, dying, all because I was too fond of my home to leave it!' The Buddha picked him up, and then addressed the villagers:

'The tortoise met his end because he was too attached to his home. Do not be like this tortoise. Do not cling to material things with desire.'

Questions

1. Who was the King of Benaras? (1 mark)

____

____

2. What was unique about the lake and the river? (2 marks)

____

____

3. Why did one tortoise not go into the river? (2 marks)

____

____

4. What did he do instead? (2 marks)

____

____

5. How did the tortoise meet his end? (2 marks)

____

____

6. Who addressed the villagers? What did he tell them? (2 marks)

____

____

7. 'In agony, the tortoise thought .....'

   a. What does 'agony' mean in this sentence?
   Select and copy **one** correct answer from
   pain   happiness   excitement   sorrow (1 mark)

   b. The Buddha was born in a __________ family.
   Choose and write **one** correct answer from
   weaver's   blacksmith's   royal   potter's (1 mark)

8. According to you, what is the moral of the story? (2 marks)

____

____

B. Read this passage about Cher Ami, a brave male pigeon gifted by Britain to the US Army Signal Corps for use in France during World War I. Then answer the questions.

In 1918, the USA's Major Whittlesey and his men were trapped behind enemy lines. They had neither food nor ammunition. Surrounded by enemies, many were injured or killed and only 194 soldiers survived.

They needed help to get away. Since his messengers were always caught or killed by the Germans, Whittlesey decide to send messages through pigeons. The first two pigeons were shot down. Then Cher Ami was sent.

When he tried to fly back home, the Germans shot him, but he took flight again. He returned to the division headquarters and thus helped save the lives of 194 soldiers.

However, he was severely wounded. He had been shot through the breast, blinded in one eye, and had a leg hanging only by a tendon.

He was awarded the prestigious French Croix de Guerre medal for his heroic deeds. On 13 June 1919, he died from the wounds he had received in the battle.

Questions

1. Who was Cher Ami? (1 mark)

2. What problems did Major Whittlesey face when he and his men were trapped behind enemy lines? (2 marks)

3. Why did Major Whittlesey need to send messages? (2 marks)

4. Why did Major Whittlesey decide to send messages through pigeons? (2 marks)

5. How severely was Cher Ami wounded? (2 marks)

6. How did Cher Ami die? (2 marks)

7. *...Major Whittlesey and his men were trapped behind enemy lines.*

   What does the word 'trapped' mean in this sentence? Look at the following words and circle the correct answer.

   stuck fought caught lost (1 mark)

8. From the information given in the passage, write about the bravery shown by Cher Ami? (3 marks)

NOTES

NOTES

NOTES